Isabel's Closet
Paper Doll and Craft Book

© Jan May 2010. All rights reserved.

Isabel's Closet by Jan May
© 2010, Jan May.
Illustrations by Julianna Davis
Graphic Design by Zandrah Kurland

All rights reserved. No part of this book may be used or reproduced in any manner whatsoever without written permission, except where noted.

www.NewMillenniumGirlBooks.com

Welcome to Isabel's Closet!

This book accompanies **The New Millennium Girls Writing Curriculum: Introducing Isabel.** There are two pages of each design and three pages of evening gowns. By using different colors, different patterns, flowers, stars, glitter, and stickers, you can create two different outfits with each one.

This book includes:
- ★ Isabel paper doll on the cover
- ★ Two Princess paper dolls inside
- ★ Paper doll stands on back cover
- ★ Sixteen pages of clothes for Isabel
- ★ Sixteen pages of clothes for the Princess
- ★ Two horses and riders
- ★ *How to Build Isabel's Bedroom* instruction pages

You may copy additional pages of doll clothes to create more designs.

Check out The New Millennium Girl's web site for fun crafts and recipes. Download the newest outfits and find out what Isabel and her best friend Holly are up to. **www.NewMillenniumGirlBooks.com**

Isabel's Closet

This is Isabel's favorite outfit when she rides Starlight through the grassy meadows.

Isabel's Closet

Isabel's Closet

Isabel's Closet

Isabel's Closet

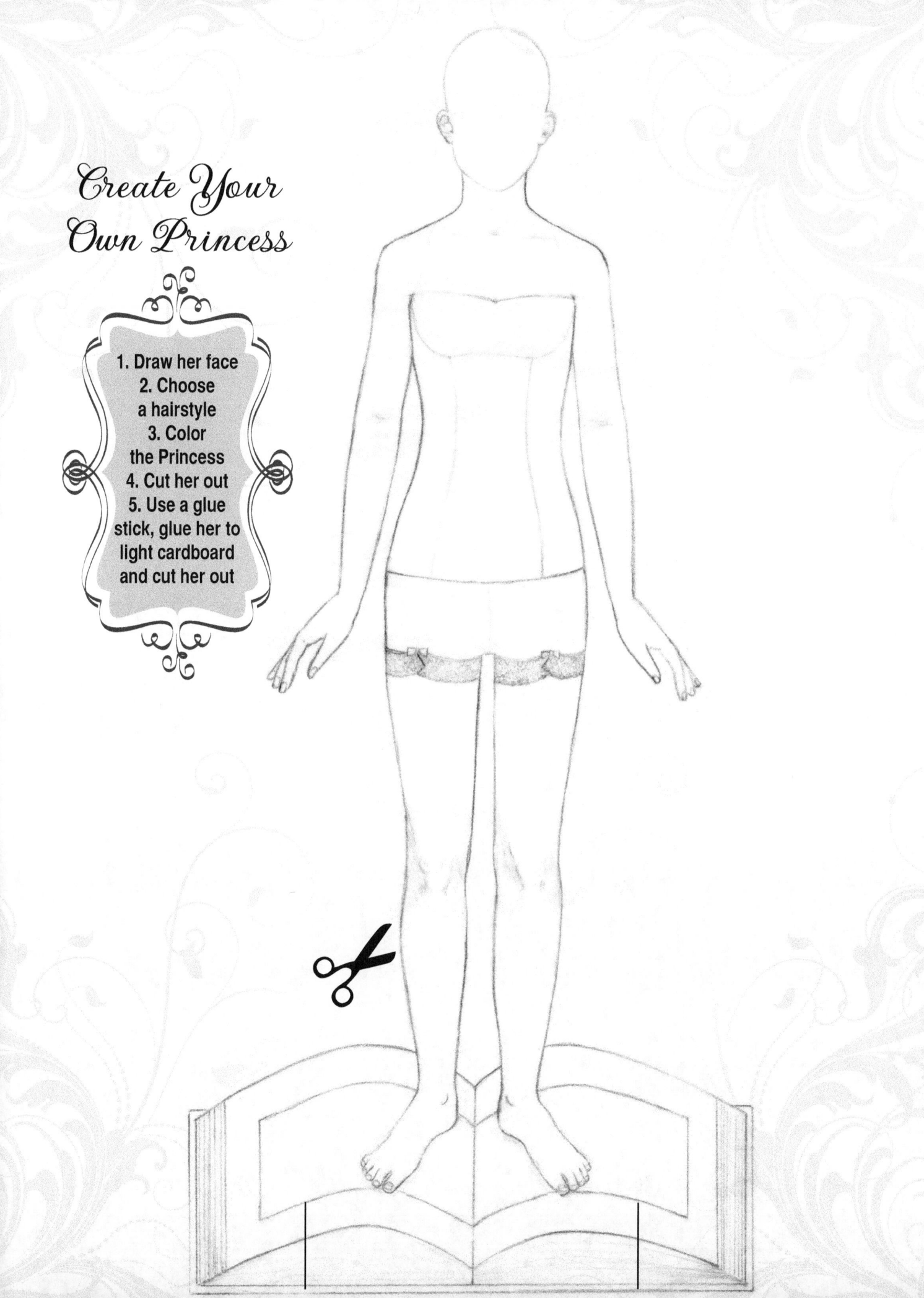

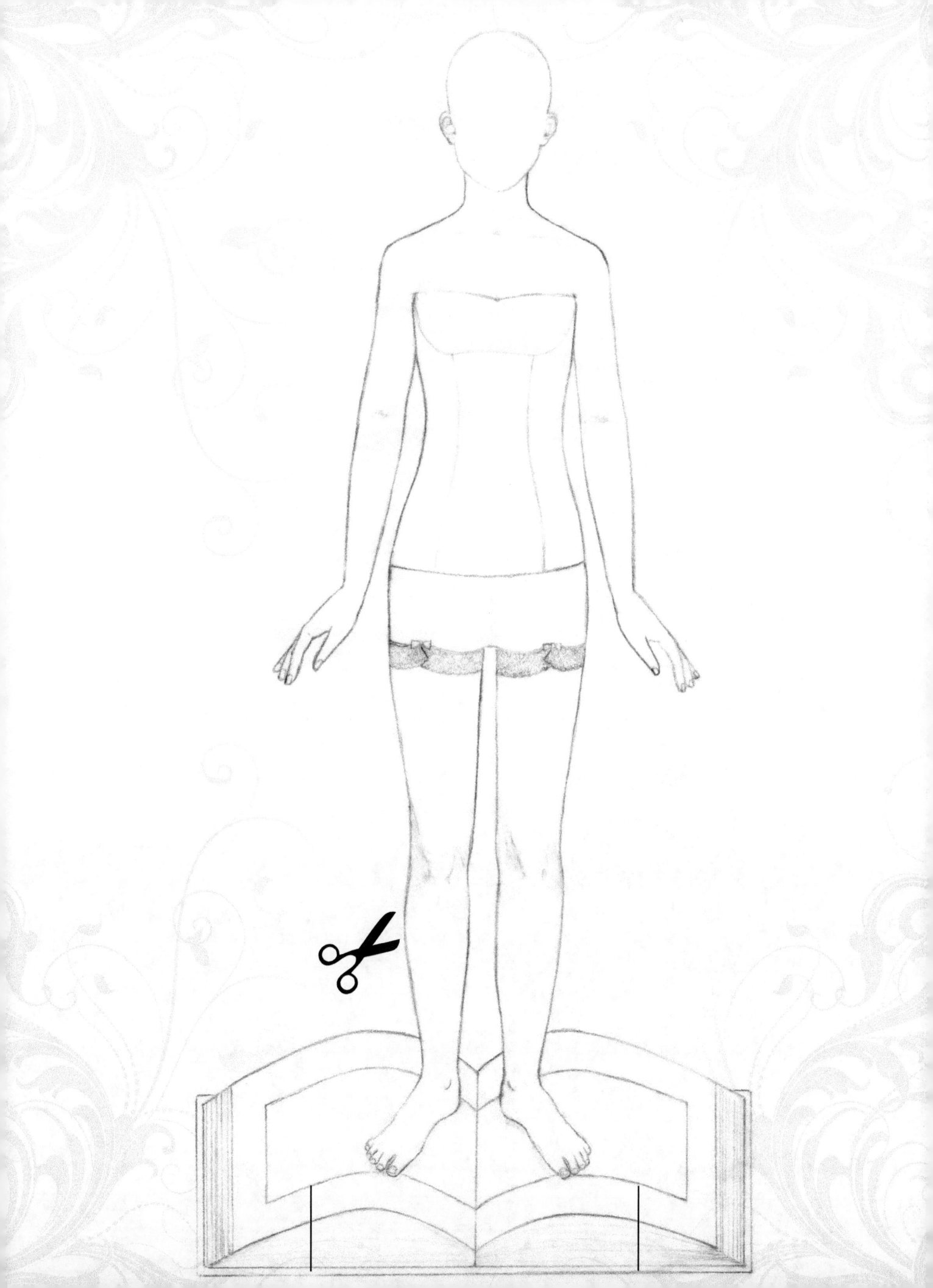

Hair Designs

Choose from curly up-dos to sleek and straight to match with the Princess's wardrobe. Color these hair designs from blonde to dark chocolate.

Hair Designs

The Princess Collection

Draw your own design by using flowers or glitter to add that sparkling look to this elegant evening dress.

The Princess Collection

The Princess Collection

Evening Wear

This is one of the Princess' favorite dresses. Give it a special flair with flowers or glitter.

Evening Wear

Evening Wear

Evening Wear

Add your own shimmer to make the Princess shine in this taylor-made evening gown.

Evening Wear

Evening Wear

Party Wear

Whether she is out with her friends to have a banana split or planning to meet her aunt for tea, the Princess can be ready with this dress. Add your own floral pattern or polka-dots to decorate it for the occasion.

Party Wear

Riding Wear

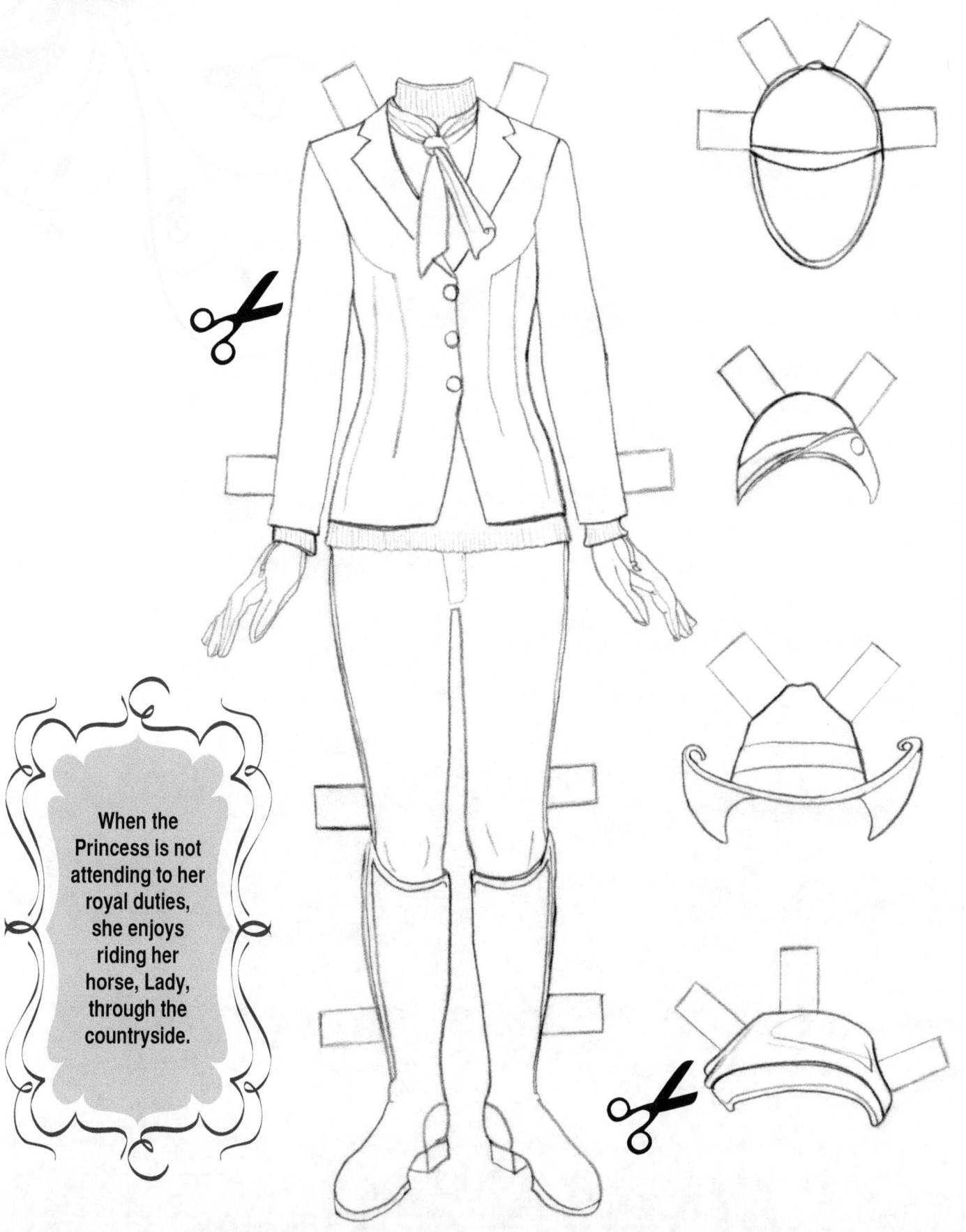

When the Princess is not attending to her royal duties, she enjoys riding her horse, Lady, through the countryside.

Riding Wear

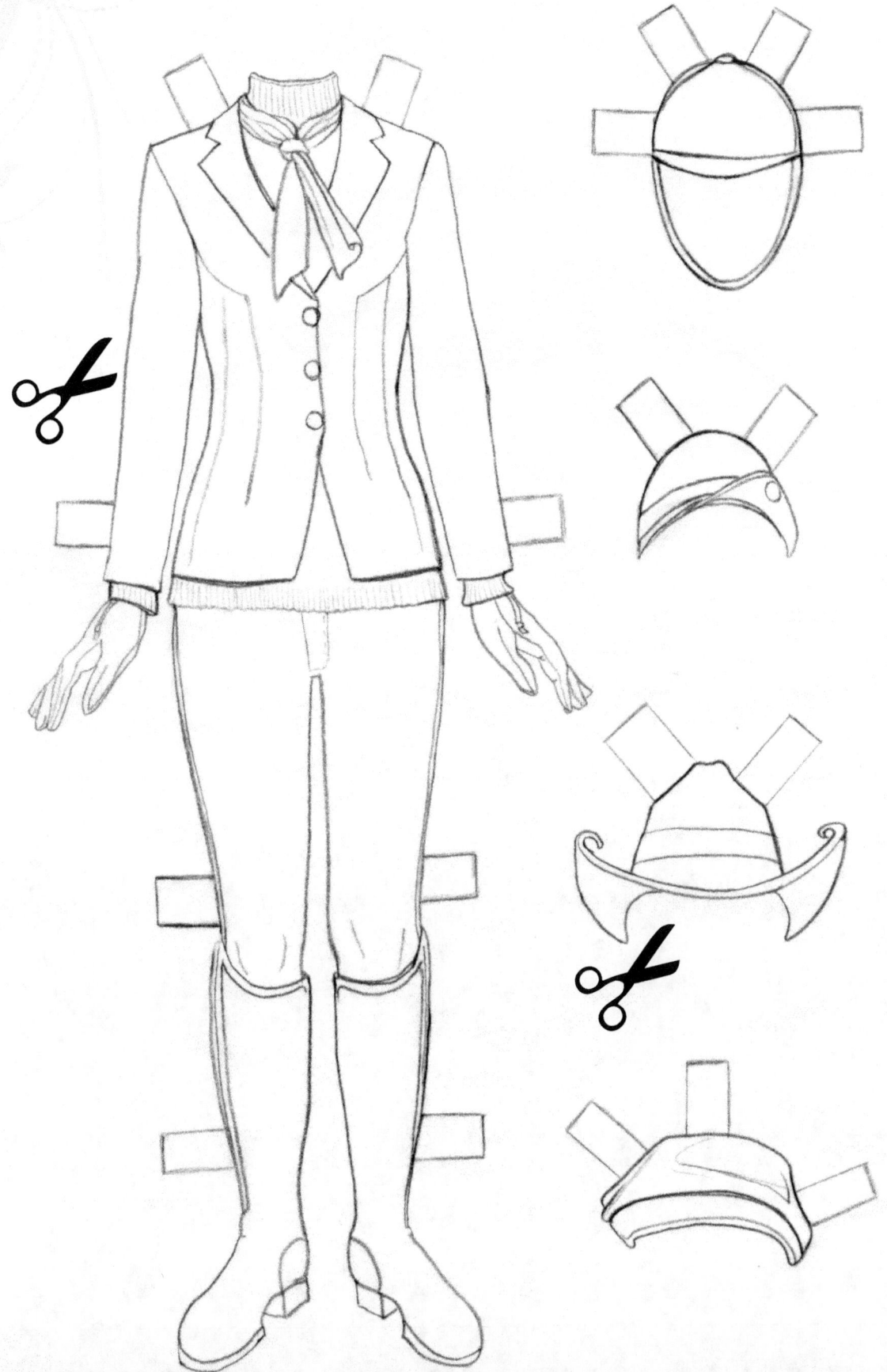

Casual Wear

Casual Wear

1. Color Isabel and Starlight.
2. Using a glue stick, glue them to light cardboard or cardstock.
3. Cut them out.
4. Cut out their stands on the back cover.
5. Bend the stand and insert into the bottom of the horse to make them stand up.

Starlight

CRAFT TIME FOR LESSON 2
Building a Closet and Bedroom for Isabel

1. Gather together:

   ★ Your fun folder
   ★ 4-6 plastic sleeves that open on top
   ★ 8-10 pieces of solid card stock any color you like 8.5 x 11 or 4-6 fun designed scrap booking papers same size
   ★ Department store magazines that have pictures of furniture in them
   ★ Glue stick and scissors

2. Slip the cardstock or papers into the top of the plastic sleeves. This will serve as a background for the closet. Leave one or two plastic sleeves empty.

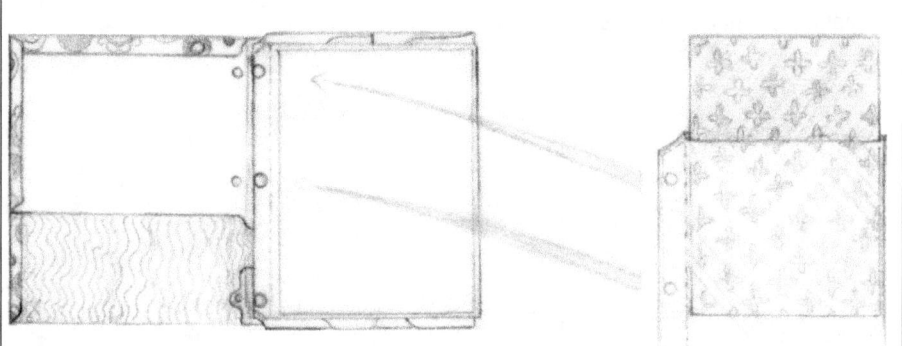

3. Cut out pictures of bedroom furniture from a magazine and glue them on a piece of 8.5 x 11 card stock and slip into one of the plastic covers. You can make a living room, too and slip it on the other side. By turning the page, you can be in another room.

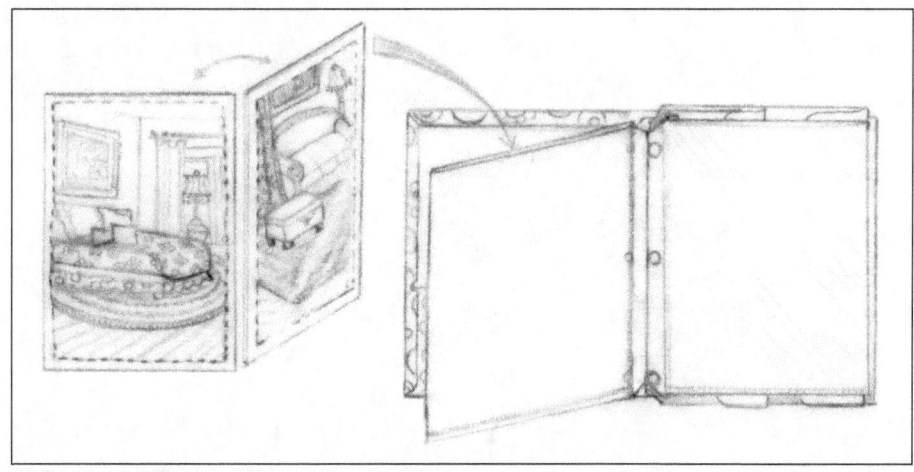

Building a Closet and Bedroom for Isabel

4. Fasten the plastic sleeves into the middle of your folder. Store the clothes you make inside the plastic sleeves.

5. For extra fun, you can add a plastic page with a zipper compartment or snap pockets.

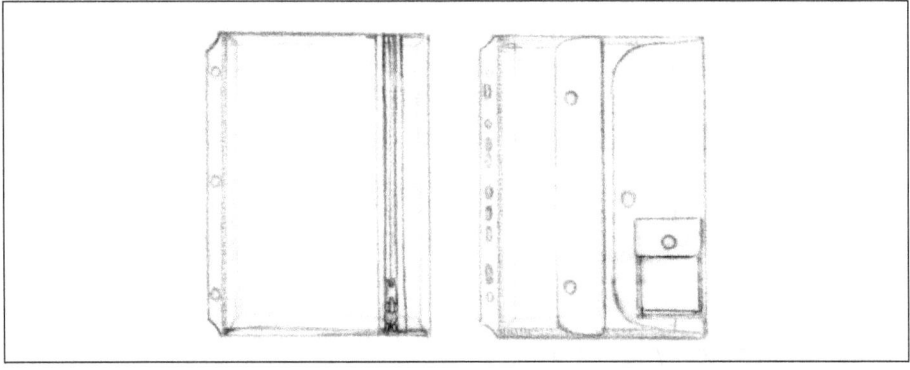

About the Author

Jan May has been teaching children to write for over fifteen years. She is the Co-Author of *Creative and Crafty Writing*-the fun way to get kids to write. She is also a graduate of the Institute of Children's Literature and has a college background in Biblical studies and Christian Education from North Central University in Minneapolis, Minnesota.

Check out the New Millennium Girl's web site for fun crafts, recipes and stories. Watch for surprise downloads of fun new outfits for Isabel and the princess.

Look for the new fiction book, *Isabel's Secret*, coming soon. Isabel Morningsky is a spirited eleven year old girl who lives on Angel Ridge Horse Ranch in Colorado. "Winners never quit and quitters never win, for I serve the mighty God that lives deep within!" This has been Isabel's motto since she was three years old. Can it help her win the annual Thanksgiving Day bareback race against Kip Johnson, even though she's a girl? Can it help her uncover the deep family secret that Grandmother Biltmore never wants her to find out? Will she survive "girl camp"? Join Isabel and her loveable horse, Starlight, as the mystery unfolds in the faith adventure: *Isabel's Secret*.

You can order this book and others at: **www.NewMillenniumGirlBooks.com**

www.ingramcontent.com/pod-product-compliance
Lightning Source LLC
Chambersburg PA
CBHW060518300426
44112CB00017B/2720